The Ever
Playbook:

Your Tactical Playbook To Be Seen Everywhere By Your Hottest Prospects

Joe Fier & Matt Wolfe are the co-founders of Evergreen Profits and absolutely LOVE showing people how simple it really is to get seen online in competitive industries. They get pumped up to share their system of driving targeted traffic that turns into leads and sales to business owners who want to scale (but have failed in the past). They aren't an agency (they're pretty much the anti-agency).

Over a combined 22 years in business, they have generated over $100 million for themselves and their clients, co-founded a startup that sold to Kodak, and have dialed in a traffic strategy that just requires a tiny budget and allows you to be seen everywhere to the people you want.

They host a well-respected and quickly growing business podcast called The Hustle And Flowchart Podcast. They interview leading experts and provide actionable takeaways, as well as entertaining conversations.

Praise for Joe & Matt

"Your traffic system is one-of-a-kind. Other systems practically require that you make getting traffic a second career, that's how complicated they are. Yours is simple but brilliant, trimming everything down to just the essentials elements that work best and work consistently. I'm a big fan of anything that lets you do a lot more with less time and effort and your systems truly delivers that."
-- Bob Serling, *Profit Alchemy*

"I have no clue how you're doing it, but you guys send loads of traffic every single day. The best part is that it converts really well and I see your ads everywhere. I need more affiliates like you guys!
-- Paul Clifford, *Designrr*

"These people are bringing some serious value. Don't be stupid, LISTEN and implement some sh*t."
-- Billy Gene, *Billy Gene Is Marketing*

"These two are savvy. Excellent implementers, entertaining and humble. I really see them going a long way. Watch this space. Also they have a great traffic course which I am halfway through."
-- James Schramko, *SuperFastBusiness*

"We bought it, you sold us. You've supported us above and beyond I've ever expected. Better than many companies

support their own business. So I appreciate that tremendously!"
-- Mike Michalowicz, *New York Times Best Selling Author*
(On how we sell & support affiliate products)

"These guys offer some of the smartest business ideas and concepts, they should be part of every entrepreneur's business life!"
-- Tripthunh, *Podcast Listener*

"Been a fan of Matt and Joe for a while and the podcast is definitely one of the ones that I go back to listen to again and again. Two guys, doing the work, been through the grind and living in the trenches. Always good info and most importantly the advice is real and actionable. Highly recommended!"
-- rtdietz, *Podcast Listener*

"Every podcast offers the listener something that will change their life and business, because when business can get easier with the great hacks and strategies, then life is sweeter. As Matt & Joe portray their real human selves tackling life and business challenges, you laugh, sometimes cry (from laughing so hard) and always leave the episode more informed than when it started."
-- FTMom5199, *Podcast Listener*

The Evergreen Traffic Playbook:

Your Tactical Playbook To Be Seen Everywhere By Your Hottest Prospects

---

Joe Fier & Matt Wolfe

Evergreen Profits, Published 2018

First Printing: 2018

ISBN 978-0-359-11994-3

Evergreen Profits
771 Jamacha Road
El Cajon, California 92019

www.EvergreenProfits.com

To Learn More from Joe Fier & Matt Wolfe, check out:

The Hustle & Flowchart Podcast:
HustleAndFlowchart.com

Additional Articles, Books,
And Online Courses:
EvergreenProfits.com

Table of Contents

Let's Get Started!

How would it feel to be top-of-mind to the people who are actively searching for your brand, hot topics in your niche, and people who visit your website? That'd be pretty awesome, right?

Well, the issue is that most people don't understand how to capture these folks when they land on their site and they don't know how to present themselves in front of them later.

Most folks also don't know how to get laser targeted with their paid and organic traffic efforts to get seen by these people in Google and other platforms.

This is SO common and something we struggled with for almost 10 years. It's TOUGH and expensive to run traffic using the methods that are taught by some of the largest traffic "gurus".

It also doesn't help that traffic and SEO agencies make you feel useless when it comes to running your own traffic that *actually* converts! That sucks!

That is why we finally created a simple book for you to follow so you can get ahead of the traffic game. We have created this book to give you our strategies of being seen "everywhere" to the right people who are engaging with us or looking up something we offer.

(Side note: These traffic strategies work for you if you have your own online business, information products, promote other people's products as an affiliate, run a brick and mortar company, have an ecommerce store with healthy profits, and any other business).

More traffic DOES NOT equal more money. Most people get that wrong.

Most people also think that running TARGETED traffic to interested people is difficult. **It's not** :-)

This is a book that was created solely for the purpose to show you that you ARE capable of running your own traffic…

That you DON'T need an expensive agency to manage everything for $2,000+ retainers per month and don't have your best profit-generating intentions as you do for your business.

This book was made to give you *actionable* strategies and steps to follow to start your traffic journey and convert interested people into buyers of your products and services.

It's not rocket science and we try to keep this simple for the non-techy and even the folks who aren't expert marketers. ANYONE with a business that has an offer and knows their numbers can use these strategies.

Ok, ok. So let's kick things off with how we get seen every single day (in very competitive niches) by people who are highly qualified and ready to buy. This is the start to a fun little journey...

How We Get Highly Qualified, Ready-to-Buy Traffic Everyday

Traffic is often a tough beast to tame...

So many people do it completely wrong... To be fair, so many people TEACH it wrong too. Here's the best advice we can possibly give...

All traffic is NOT created equal. Different traffic sources serve different roles.

So many people go straight to Facebook and try to use that one platform to drive all of their traffic back to their site.

They don't make sales quickly and they give up.

The problem is that Facebook is not a place where people hang out that are looking for something to buy.

However, on Google, when someone searches for "best chiropractor" or "best email opt-in tool", there's a pretty damn good chance that they're looking to spend money.

So here's how we use advertising (here's a summary before getting into details)...

We create an ad on Google, based on what they're looking to buy... We target people that might search "best email opt-in tool" and we put an article in front of them.

This article can be a review of various tools, a tutorial around one tool, or something that helps make the sale of the tool.

THEN, and only after they clicked our article, do we start retargeting people on other platforms like Facebook and Google.

They've shown interest because they did the search. They're now familiar with our solution because they read our article. And now they're seeing us everywhere like we have a monster ad budget because we're retargeting them everywhere.

This traffic flow works like crazy and is the reason we're as successful as we are today.

Have you been struggling to drive highly qualified traffic to your website or offers?

Most people seem to be able to either drive a lot of traffic that doesn't convert into sales very well or they haven't managed to crack that nut on how to drive traffic in the first place.

In this deep-dive post, I'm going to walk you through how we drive traffic that's reliable, consistent, and very qualified… Meaning that the traffic that we send actually buys stuff.

We've taught this strategy on two other occasions… The first time was in an, invite-only, mastermind where people paid $3k each to be in the room. The other time was when we briefly discussed it on this podcast episode (https://evergreenprofits.com/effectivetraffic).

The podcast episode was a good primer but, today we're going to go a little deeper down the rabbit hole.

So let's begin…

The Typical Way People Drive Traffic:

Here's how most people drive traffic with Facebook ads...

They create their offer page, they go to their Facebook ads dashboard, they find a bunch of targets that they think would be relevant and add them to an adset, and they point this traffic to their offer page. They

4

hope that the combination of interest targets, ad images, ad copy, and landing page converts a small percentage of the people that see the page into sales.

The problem with this approach is that people don't go on Facebook to buy things. People are on Facebook to see what their friends and family are up to and to see how many likes their most recent vacation photo got them. Your ad is interrupting that experience for them and you have no real idea if the interest targets you selected are actually people that would want what you're offering. More than likely, they liked a page a couple of years ago, forgot they liked it, and now their seeing your ad which may or may not still be relevant to where they are in life right now.

Now, here's how most people drive traffic with Google search ads...

They create their offer page, login to the Adwords dashboard, create search ads for people who search their product name or who search for a competing product's name. They may sprinkle in some broad keywords as well that are relevant to what they're selling and hope that it pans out for them.

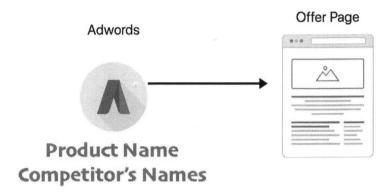

Adwords

Offer Page

Product Name
Competitor's Names

The problem with this approach to Google ads is that you're mostly targeting "solution aware" people. The people that are going to see your ad are people that are already aware that your product exists or, at the very least, a competitor's product exists. This is great and you should definitely scoop up that traffic, however, you're not really getting your offer in front of new eyeballs that may have no clue that you're the answer to their problems.

If you've ever run Google ads before, you probably also know that going after broad keywords can be very expensive and often lead to a lot of clicks that really aren't your ideal customer.

Yes, there are some people that get lucky and the above methods work just fine and get them of a nice ROI. However, we like a little more certainty than that. We like to know that only the most relevant people are seeing our ads... and seeing them often.

That's why we pieced together our own little traffic strategy... A strategy that we call The Perpetual Audience Growth Formula. It's a mashup of strategies from about ten other marketers that we pieced together to build the ultimate traffic tactic. It drives consistent results and is easily predictable.

Now, before I go any further… This strategy is NOT for everybody.

If you're unwilling to spend money to grow your business, this will not be for you. It relies heavily on paid advertising and a few key premium tools. Anyone with an aversion to investing money to get their business going, look elsewhere.

If you have nothing to promote, this is not for you. This isn't a simple *"make money online"* scheme. This is a way to drive qualified traffic to existing offers.

If you have a product that is crap, this isn't for you. No amount of great marketing is going to help you sell a product that people just don't want.

This strategy DOES work for:

- Information marketers who sell online courses

- Coaches and consultants who have a specific focus

- Ecommerce businesses who operate in a specific niche

- Software / SaaS companies – We've seen MASSIVE results here

- Brick and mortar businesses who want more leads

- Trade specialists – Doctors, plumbers, lawyers, electricians, etc.

- **Affiliate marketers** – We use this strategy to generate thousands per day in profits, promoting affiliate offers.

I'm sure there are other areas that this works for but those are the ones that we've specifically worked with people to help build in the past.

If you're not running ads already, we'll show you how to do it right, from the start… If you are running ads already, this will show you how to tie everything together between Google, Facebook, and any other ad platforms you want to play with.

The Traffic Strategy In A Nutshell:

Step 1:

Start by trying to think of things that people would search who have the problem that your product solves. Think of long-tail keywords and not really broad keywords.

For example, if you're a plumber, think of keywords people would search for where your services would help. "How to fix a leaky faucet" or "How to unclog a toilet when plunger isn't working". I'm not a plumber so I don't have the best examples. However, the simplest way to do this is to go to Google and start typing in some keywords and seeing what Google autofills in.

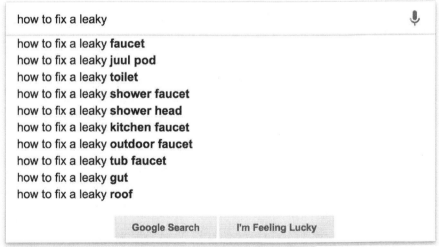

Let's say you have a software solution that writes email copy for people... What things would people search for that are long-tail keywords people might search that your solution can help?

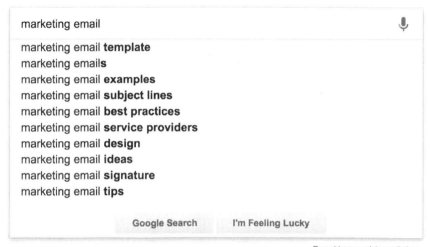

Google's suggestion will be a good start to find some of these keywords. As you dive deeper into the process, there are several other ways to find keywords to target.

However, this first step gives us ideas of things that people are searching for where your solution can shortcut the distance between their problem and their goal.

Step 2:

Once you have 5 or 6 long-tail keywords that you want to start with, create a piece of content for each of them. It can be a podcast episode, a written blog post, a video, or some combination. We personally often hire a writer from the Problogger Jobs board to write us a handful of articles around the keywords we give them. You can do whatever works best for you and your flow to get some content out.

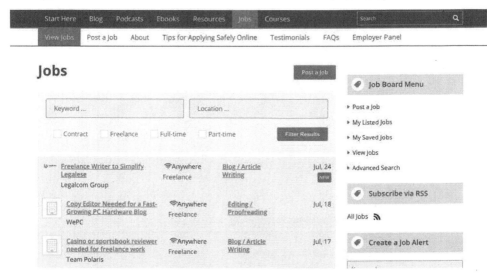

Publish these articles to your blog (we like self-hosted WordPress blogs). We'll be using these articles to initially drive traffic to.

Step 3:

In Google Adwords, create a campaign for each article and write ads promoting each blog post. We typically like to create one campaign for each country we're targeting as well. That way, if it works well in one country, we can scale by duplicating the campaign in another country.

Example for a plumber:

- Campaign: "How to fix a leaky faucet – US"

- Ad group #1: Keywords: [How to fix a leaky faucet] [Fix a leaky faucet] etc.

- Ads: Create at least 2 relevant text ads for the article so that you're always testing

So the campaign is always the main keyword for the article. The ad groups within that campaign are based on the keywords you're targeting. I put them in brackets "[ ]" because that tells Google that we only want the ad to show up if they search that exact term in that order. For the ads, always have 2 ads running so that you can constantly split test and beat the current control.

Create a campaign:

Type: Search

| Campaign name | How to fix a leaky faucet - US | ∧ |

Networks

Search Network

Ads can appear near Google Search results and other Google sites when people search for terms that are relevant to your keywords

☐ Include Google search partners ⑦

Display Network

Expand your reach by showing ads to relevant customers as they browse sites, videos, and apps across the Internet

☐ Include Google Display Network ⑦

Locations

Select locations to target ⑦

○ All countries and territories
○ United States and Canada
◉ United States
○ Enter another location

🔍 Enter a location to target or exclude   Advanced search

For example, a country, city, region, or postal code

∨ Location options

Languages

Select the languages your customers speak ⑦

English ⊗

🔍 Start typing or select a language

12

Create your ad groups:

Create your ads:

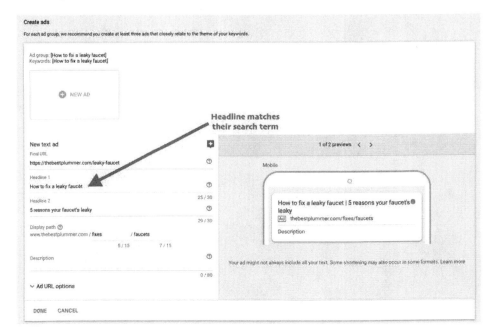

Step 4:

Create retargeting ads on Facebook and Google Display Network and point people to your offer.

We basically use Facebook ads and GDN solely for retargeting. Remember, I mentioned that if we use interest targeting on Facebook, we're probably interrupting people with an ad that's probably not super relevant. However, if we retarget people who viewed a piece of content that was related to their problem, we know that this offer is super relevant to them. We used the initial Google ad and blog post to get people to "raise their hands" and say "I've got this problem that I need solved" and now, with retargeting, we're putting the solution to their problem right in front of their face.

From a prospect from it looks kinda like this:

- My faucet is leaking – I'm gonna Google it and see what my options are

- See an article – "5 reasons your faucet is leaking"

- Later that day, they're on Facebook or some random blog and they see an ad: "The simple solution to leaky faucets – Get in touch with Bob the plumber"

- The prospect thinks in their mind "whoa – how did this random ad know I needed a plumber?"

- Prospect revisits your site – This time to your offer page

- Prospect calls you because the ad they just saw was timed amazingly

That flow works with pretty much any business… Just replace the blog article and ad content with what's relevant to your business.

You get them to "raise their hand" and tell the ad networks they have a problem that needs solving through search ads and quality content. You follow the "hand raisers" around the internet with your offer to fix their problem.

Here's a simplified version of this new advertising flow:

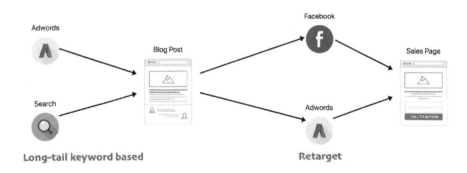

When done correctly, this honestly gets people thinking that you're inside their head. Everything looks so well timed and your ads just seem like they're popping up at the right place at the right time.

Why "The Perpetual Audience Growth Formula?"

I know the name is a bit of a mouthful. At Evergreen Profits, we simply call it a "P.A.G." We find ourselves saying to each other, "let's run a PAG to the offer and see how it performs."

We call it that because, while you are driving a lot of traffic, you are, more importantly, building audiences that you can tap again and again in the future.

This strategy will grow your list. If you have opt-in forms on your blog, you'll see your list skyrocket. These are people you can mail over and over again with new content and new offers.

This strategy builds out Facebook retargeting audiences with qualified prospects. You can run ads to this audience whenever you want.

This strategy builds out your Google remarketing audiences with qualified prospects that you can get in front of over and over again.

This strategy grows your Facebook fan page. As people see your ads on Facebook, more and more of them will like your page, giving you access to promote organic and paid content to them.

This strategy grows your brand and name recognition. It will appear to the people that enter your ad ecosystem that you have a massive ad budget. They'll see you everywhere.

Real Life Example:

We acquired a company that teaches you how to get better sleep at night and we rebranded it as SolidRest.com.

We used a keyword research tool to find a ton of keywords related to common searches around sleep.

One of the common things that seemed to pop up a lot and that had a lot of search volume was searches related to the best mattress pads to get a better night's sleep. People searching for the kind of thing are likely looking for other solutions to fall asleep as well.

So, we hired a writer to create an article called "Can Mattress Pads Improve The Quality Of Your Sleep?"

HOME   BUY COURSE   LOGIN   CONTACT   Q

CAN MATTRESS PADS IMPROVE THE QUALITY OF YOUR SLEEP?

1 month ago

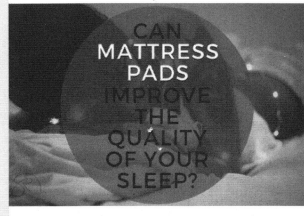

CAN
MATTRESS
PADS
IMPROVE
THE
QUALITY
OF YOUR
SLEEP?

What is life without good quality sleep? Miserable at best. It's common to lay blame on lifestyle habits and your sleep environment when you're missing out on quality

SOLID REST COURSE

SOLID REST

FREE SLEEP AUDIOS

Free Gift
7
BEST
AUDIOS TO
HELP YOU
FALL ASLEEP
EFFORTLESSLY
Click here

We then created a Google ad campaign around that keyword…

☐ ●   Want Better Sleep At Night?
Learn How Mattress Pads Help
www.solidrest.com
Mattress pads can help you get a better night
sleep. Read this to learn more.

☐ ●   Mattress Pads For Better Sleep
This Blog Post Explains How
www.solidrest.com
Mattress pads can help you get a better night
sleep. Read this to learn more.

Notice that we created two variations so that we can eventually turn off the loser and create a new variation to try to beat the previous winner.

We also created a Facebook retargeting ad and a Google Display Network ad that would then follow people around after they visited the article.

Now, when you search for mattress pads as a way to get a better night sleep (and when you're in our target location), you'll see an ad to our blog post. When you click on the blog post, you will see our ads everywhere that link you to the offer to get our sleep course.

Some of Our Results:

We've managed to dial this in so well that we use it to promote offers as affiliates, we use it to promote our own internal products, and we've helped set it up for clients.

Here's a screenshot from one of the affiliate promotions that we've been running on an ongoing basis:

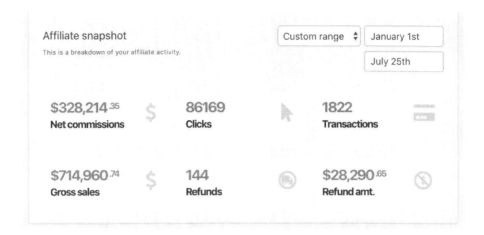

Here's an actual look inside one of the affiliate platforms, showing that we generate sales every. single. day.:

Type	Date	Product name	Amount	
Commission	07/25/18 10:46pm		$297.50 USD	stripe
Commission	07/25/18 10:46pm		$49.50 USD	stripe
Commission	07/25/18 4:24pm		$297.50 USD	stripe
Commission	07/25/18 1:07pm		$297.50 USD	PayPal
Commission	07/25/18 1:07pm		$49.50 USD	PayPal
Commission	07/25/18 4:16am		$297.50 USD	stripe
Commission	07/25/18 12:41am		$297.50 USD	stripe
Commission	07/24/18 11:26pm		$297.50 USD	stripe
Commission	07/24/18 10:52pm		$13.50 USD	PayPal
Commission	07/24/18 8:38pm		$13.50 USD	stripe

Type	Date	Product name	Amount	
Commission	07/24/18 4:13pm		$297.50 USD	PayPal
Commission	07/24/18 2:23pm		$297.50 USD	stripe
Commission	07/24/18 2:03pm		$13.50 USD	PayPal
Commission	07/23/18 4:51pm		$297.50 USD	stripe
Commission	07/23/18 4:51pm		$47.50 USD	stripe
Commission	07/23/18 3:11pm		$13.50 USD	stripe
Commission	07/23/18 12:28am		$297.50 USD	stripe
Commission	07/23/18 12:28am		$49.50 USD	stripe
Commission	07/22/18 4:49pm		$297.50 USD	stripe
Commission	07/21/18 5:28pm		$297.50 USD	stripe

Type	Date	Product name	Amount	
Commission	07/21/18 5:28pm		$49.50 USD	stripe
Commission	07/21/18 11:15am		$9.50 USD	PayPal
Commission	07/20/18 8:10pm		$297.50 USD	stripe
Commission	07/20/18 8:10pm		$49.50 USD	stripe
Commission	07/20/18 4:50pm		$297.50 USD	PayPal
Commission	07/20/18 6:19am		$297.50 USD	PayPal
Commission	07/20/18 6:19am		$49.50 USD	PayPal
Commission	07/20/18 5:24am		$297.50 USD	stripe
Commission	07/20/18 1:53am		$297.50 USD	PayPal
Commission	07/19/18 5:49pm		$297.50 USD	stripe

This isn't during a launch, this isn't from a special promo, this isn't even from us mailing our list. These are sales that come in from multiple different products that we promote as affiliates. They're consistent, they're reliable, we can forecast this month and the next month, and we know it's not slowing down.

This is purely from a few PAG campaigns that we set up around different affiliate products. We can take any random sample of any week and it looks similar…

Here's a screenshot of an affiliate offer we promoted that uses Infusionsoft. (The screenshot was massive so I cut the middle) You can see that it generates fairly consistent reliable sales…

Commissions Earned For Date Range (01-01-2018 - 07-25-2018)

Inv#	Date	Contact	SoldBy	Item	Amount
#16743	1/4/2018	C	David Francis		$57.70
#16767	1/5/2018	J	Matthew Wolfe		$198.80
#16771	1/5/2018	D	Matthew Wolfe		$198.80
#16843	1/9/2018	R	Matthew Wolfe		$173.10
#16883	1/10/2018	J	Matthew Wolfe		$149.10
#16999	1/12/2018	T	Matthew Wolfe		$173.10
#17073	1/14/2018	P	Matthew Wolfe		$173.10
#17083	1/14/2018	D	Matthew Wolfe		$89.46
#17237	1/15/2018	S	Matthew Wolfe		$173.10
#17293	1/16/2018	S	Matthew Wolfe		$173.10
#17633	1/21/2018	P	Matthew Wolfe		$173.10
#17831	1/29/2018	J	Matthew Wolfe	se	$149.10
#22614	6/12/2018	S	Matthew Wolfe		$26.70
#22624	6/12/2018	E	Matthew Wolfe		$125.28
#22628	6/12/2018	A	Matthew Wolfe		$26.70
#22792	6/15/2018	M	Matthew Wolfe		$177.48
#22842	6/17/2018	A	amoci ses P.iva 03648490	Matthew Wolfe	$23.40
#22844	6/17/2018	H	dgens	Matthew Wolfe	$11.70
#22940	6/19/2018	R	Matthew Wolfe		$11.70
#23036	6/21/2018	J	RY	Matthew Wolfe	$26.70
#23040	6/21/2018	S	Matthew Wolfe		$23.40
#23078	6/22/2018	K	Matthew Wolfe		$26.70
#23280	6/27/2018	J	Matthew Wolfe		$11.70
#23456	7/1/2018	T	Matthew Wolfe		$26.70
#23518	7/3/2018	P	Matthew Wolfe		$26.70
#23562	7/5/2018	T	Matthew Wolfe		$11.70
#23588	7/5/2018	C	Matthew Wolfe		$177.48
#23650	7/7/2018	G	Matthew Wolfe		$23.40
#23586	7/7/2018	C	Matthew Wolfe		$177.48
#23860	7/12/2018	B	Matthew Wolfe		$11.70
#23862	7/12/2018	S	Matthew Wolfe		$26.70
#23870	7/12/2018	A	Matthew Wolfe		$26.70
#23996	7/17/2018	H	dgens	Matthew Wolfe	$11.70
#24080	7/19/2018	R	Matthew Wolfe		$11.70
#24084	7/19/2018	H	Matthew Wolfe		$177.48
#24170	7/21/2018	J	RY	Matthew Wolfe	$26.70
#24174	7/21/2018	S	Matthew Wolfe		$23.40
#24236	7/23/2018	J	Matthew Wolfe		$26.70
#24238	7/23/2018	S	Matthew Wolfe		$26.70
#24204	7/24/2018	K	Matthew Wolfe		$26.70

24

Here's a screenshot inside of SamCart for one of the products that we promote with this strategy… Each little blue line represents sales volume for that day…

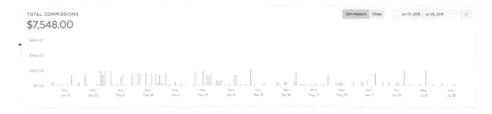

And of course, we sell a lot of our own products as well… It's not all affiliate stuff.

And the people we've been working with are taking notice too!...

Bob Serling  6:12 PM (17 hours ago) ☆ ↰ ▾

to me, Matt ▾

Your traffic system is one of a kind. Other systems practically require that you make getting traffic a second career, that's how complicated they are. Yours is simple but brilliant, trimming everything down to just the essential elements that work best and work consistently. I'm a big fan of anything that lets you do a lot more with less time and effort and your system truly delivers that.

 Brad Costanzo 5:07 PM 😊 ✉ ⇨ ☆ ⋯

Yo, Matt & Joe, I have to give you guys some major credit here, your Perpetual Audience Growth strategy is some of the most effective and advanced traffic strategies I've ever seen. Started testing it on some of my offers and my clients and finally got cold traffic to work again.... and profitably!

It's advanced, but pretty simple. Which is good for a guy like me! LOL

Now quit teaching other people this stuff!

        Markian Sich   6:57 PM

"I finally found a business and marketing course that gets me amped simply because of how fresh and unique the content is... I actually WANT to crush through every lesson as soon as possible and implement everything immediately. Thanks to Joe and Matt's guidance, my company's entire marketing direction shifted. Building a business while active duty military is NOT easy, but Joe and Matt reveal the exact steps towards growing and leveraging your traffic to increase profits and sustain them passively."

♥ 1

Tom Augenthaler
February 25

Hey everyone, thought say hi and introduce myself too. I've been following Matt for a while now and have always loved his content. Its helped me out quite a bit. About six months ago I decided to pull out all the stops and start my own online business. I'm in the Facebook ad testing phase now. Overall, I'll just tell you that starting your own business is nerve wracking, especially when you have a big monthly nut to meet (mortgage, expenses, property taxes, etc.). The cash draw down has been harsh and the retooling of my skills has taken far longer than I anticipated. I often wake up at night with "the sweats" and I often fight the feelings of self doubt. So, when I saw Matt had teamed up with Joe to start EPL, I thought it would be a good investment. After watching the video with Joe Huchison and listening to his advice about Facebook ad targeting I've already received a dividend to my investment here. I'll be implementing some of that knowledge shortly. So, thanks Matt and Joe!

Want To Go Deeper Down The Rabbit Hole?

Are you interested in building a system that consistently finds you new, high-quality, leads?

Are you interested in build a traffic strategy that you can basically create once but pretty much always works with minimal maintenance?

Are you interested in REALLY uncovering what your prospects are searching for that leads to sales of your products?

We actually created an in-depth, step-by-step, over-the-shoulder, course that walks you through every little detail of setting this up.

In fact, we set this up with a real live site that we're driving traffic to right now. It's not demo content. It's training that was created while I was building one of these actual systems that we actually drive traffic with today.

We've never sold this course. It's never been publicly available.

Until now, the only way to get access was to be one of our private consulting clients and to pay us $5k or more to directly work with us.

In all honesty, we built this and NEVER planned on selling it. It was meant to be given to our clients so that we didn't have to repeat the strategy over and over again to each new client. They could get on the phone with us and we could point them to this training in order to get their traffic dialed in.

As of this writing, only about 10 people EVER have seen the course.

However, we are finally making it publicly available!

Here's what the course looks like:

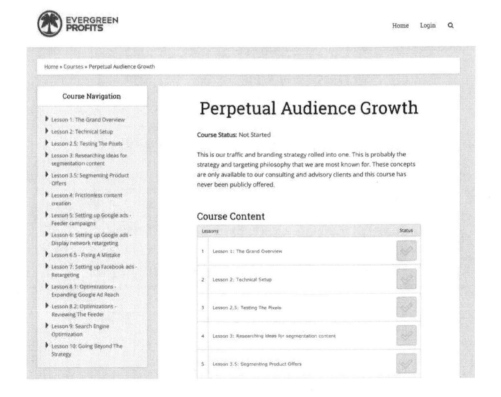

And here's a little "teaser" shot:

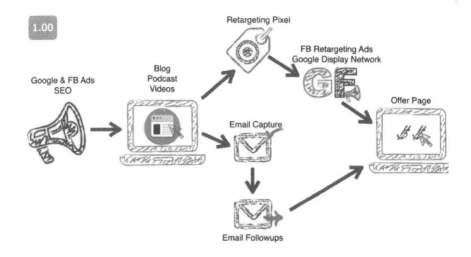

The modules aren't super long either. They are quick, to the point, and literally tell you where to click, what to do next, and why you're doing what you're doing. We keep it simple, we minimized the overwhelm, and made it so simple that anyone could follow along.

However, we wanted to make sure that you were covered and that if you did have any questions, we'd get you taken care of!

So, by grabbing this course, you'll also going to get our personal support. You'll get access to not only us, but our entire community of members. We're all there to help answer any questions you have along the way and help you scale your traffic efforts.

This isn't one of those trainings where we wish you good luck once you get in… we'll be in there with you working together and making sure this becomes a success for you!

Home

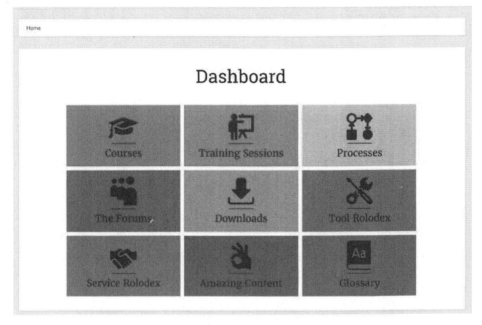

Dashboard

We'd love to have you as a member of our portal and to receive in-depth access to the traffic training. We login and we work personally with all of the members to have them overcome roadblocks and to get their traffic cranking.

So here's the deal…

The Perpetual Audience Growth Course has only been available, until now, to our consulting clients… Most who paid $5,000 minimum to access this training. We recently added it into the Portal and made it available on its own because we've had an overwhelming amount of people ask us about this stuff.

If you're interested in learning the exact process that we use every day to drive traffic to any offer (yours or someone else's), then definitely head over to this page that explains everything in detail. You can get started today…

We're legitimately only making this available because so many people have asked for it and we decided it was easier to sell a few serious entrepreneurs on accessing the training we've made than to explain it over and over again.

This stuff works, every day, for us and for our clients.

You can go here to read exactly about the Perpetual Audience Growth system and join here (spots are limited):

https://evergreenprofits.com/trafficvideo

And if you have any questions or are on the fence about this program, feel free to shoot us a message here:
https://evergreenprofits.com/trafficquestions

We are in live chat everyday and will make sure this is the right move for you.

How To Systematically Create A Never-Ending Traffic Source

Evergreen Traffic Strategy #2

Google's algorithms change. Facebook can shut you down. Ad networks can decline your ads. So how do you stay safe? Build your own audience and traffic source that you can tap into whenever you want... Here's exactly how (step-by-step).

Knowing how to drive traffic is a wonderful thing.

Once you control the flow of eyeballs to anything on the web, a whole new world of income opportunity arises for you.

If you can point loads of traffic anywhere, you can drive people to affiliate offers and earn commissions without customer support headaches.

You can drive people to your latest and greatest product or service, you can make good content go viral, or you can even drum up support for a cause or a mission.

Controlling eyeballs on the internet is a powerful thing. There are so many ways that you can take control of eyeballs as well.

You can pay for them through Google ads or Facebook ads. You can create amazing content and work on your search engine optimization so that Google will send you free traffic...

Or you can do what we do and focus on building an owned audience.

What Is An Owned Audience?

These are audiences that you can tell where to go "at will" and almost instantly drive traffic to something.

An owned audience could be something like your email list, a direct mail list, a Facebook fan page, Facebook groups, Instagram followings, and even Facebook retargeting audiences.

These are the main audiences that we focus on.

Some other amazing platforms include LinkedIn, Pinterest, YouTube, and Snapchat.

However, we don't have a ton of experience with those so we're not going to dive into those in this post.

For us, it's been all about the email list, the direct mail list, and the various Facebook opportunities.

Pick one or two of the following strategies to focus on first and get really good at it:

Build your own audience with one platform that jumps out at you (we recommend email) and then leverage that platform to grow another owned audience.

That's the beauty of building a large audience on one platform.

You can now begin to direct eyeballs from there to whatever platform you'd like to grow next.

With SEO, Google can change the algorithm and your site could disappear from search in an instant.

With advertising, you can get an account shut down or quickly run up an ad spend with no results to show for it.

Building owned audiences means that you have control over the traffic source, not some algorithm or some random person in charge of approving or denying advertising.

Next, I'm going to rapid-fire several ideas and strategies that you can use to grow your own owned audience.

The Tried And True, Most Effective Way We've Grown Our Mailing List

I'm going to start off with one that may seem obvious to some but brand new to others. However, this is still the quickest way that we've found to successfully grow our mailing list.

It's the simple opt-in page, followed by a one-time-offer, with Facebook ads to drive traffic. It's so simple but so effective.

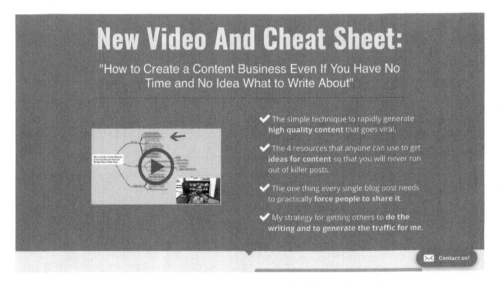

In the past, we've discussed the YouTube Curation product test method where you'd essentially create a basic opt-in page and, after they opt-in, send them to a pre-existing YouTube video.

You'd drive ad traffic to it and you'd test a product idea as well start building your list.

This strategy is essentially the same except for two major differences.

You are opting them in for something that you created and you are putting an offer for sale after they opt-in.

Theoretically, you could use someone else's video as the opt-in freebie but we want to create as much congruence as possible between what they are opting-in for and what product you have for sale.

The product that's for sale is simply there to try to recoup your costs of the advertising so that you can essentially build the list for free.

Here's a quick breakdown:

- Create some sort of free offer… 1 page "cheat sheets" seem to work well. Long videos, ebooks, or mini-courses don't seem to be that effective due to short attention spans and people not feeling like they'll get value from a free offer. Make it quick and to the point.

- Create an opt-in page using Clickfunnels or LeadPages where they can opt-in for that freebie. Simple pages work best.

- Create a sales page with a short sales video for a product priced between $47 - $97. This is the page they will see immediately after opting-in. The goal of this page is to make back some of the money from advertising.

- Use your autoresponder (we use Drip) to deliver the free guide that they opted-in for.

- Use Facebook ads to drive people to the page.

This is the tried and true strategy that we've seen work over and over again to grow our list.

We pretty much always have an ad and an offer like this running on Facebook since we're essentially breaking even on ad costs and our list is always growing. It's a free mailing list.

How To Leverage Other People's Content And Other People's Platforms To Grow Your Own Profitable Mailing List

We recently launched our new podcast and, as part of the promotion, we offered up a "teaser strategy" in exchange for subscribing and reviewing. This is actually our second most effective strategy, after the one that was mentioned above.

Here's how this works:

1. To start things off, you are going to create a blog post on your own WordPress website. In this post, you are going to make a list of "The Top 10 Articles About X". X is, of course, something that relates to your niche. 10 is an arbitrary number. In fact, the more articles that you round up, the better.

2. When someone lands on your site, you are going to have a pop-up or a little slide-in where someone can download the entire article for free (in exchange for them opting-in to your email list).

3. Finally, you are going to reach out to every single person who wrote one of the articles you mentioned and let them know that you mentioned them. That's it… that's the whole strategy.

Here's what this looks like in practice…

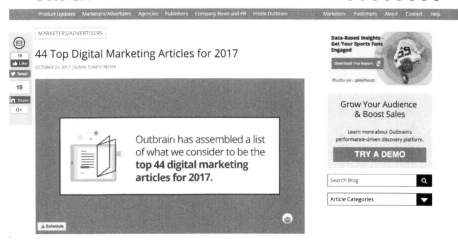

This works because people love to see themselves or their websites talked about on other sites.

Most people are more than happy to share articles with their owned audience that share kind words about them or what they're doing.

We've heard it called "share bait", "ego bait", and even "induced viral marketing." Whatever you want to call it, it's damn effective and we even use it to a small degree on every article we release now.

You'll have a hard time finding an article from us that doesn't at least mention someone else or a company. That's because we know we'll get some extra shares just for including them.

Here's What You'll Need:

- WordPress - To write content pieces on your own site.

- A Resource For Good Articles - We like Buzzsumo but you can pick from any blogs that you frequent as well.

- Designrr - To create a PDF version of the post.

- OptinMonster - To create slide-in email captures.

- Drip - To collect emails and to mail the list.

Here are the steps to accomplish this:

1. Write a blog post and title it "The Top X Articles About Y." You can get creative with the title if you'd like but that's the basic subject line that you want. X equals the number of articles you're going to share and Y equals your niche.

2. Find at least 10 articles to curate on this blog post. We personally try to think of a handful of influencers who we'd love sharing my content. We then search their blog for the content that's closest related to my topic.

3. After we have a handful that way, we'd head over to BuzzSumo and type in my niche to see what content has gotten the most shares lately, related to my topic.

4. Optionally, you can add some extra commentary to each article on your list. We typically like to link out to the article and then write a one or two sentence comment about that article to add a personal touch. Explain why it's one of your choices as a top article.

5. Install the OptinMonster plugin so that you can add a slide-in opt-in form to your blog to collect emails. Follow the instructions with the plugin to sync it to your autoresponder. We use Drip for our autoresponder. This will allow you to keep a database of the emails and mass mail them in the future.

6. Use Designrr to create a PDF version of the blog post once it's live. Simply open Designrr, copy and paste the URL of your blog post into it, and it will spit out a PDF version. You can also add some additional links or commentary to the bonus PDF to make it even more valuable to those that download it.

7. Use Drip to have the PDF version automatically sent out whenever someone opts-in to your email list.

8. Finally, chase up all of the content creators that you mentioned in your article and let them know that you mentioned them in your list. Be sure to send them a link to the blog post and ask if they know of any other articles that would make a good fit for the list. Hopefully, the professionals that you mentioned in your post will share your piece with their owned audience.

This blog post doesn't need to be a "one and done" strategy.

You can continually add new articles as you find them and follow up with the writers once they go live.

Asking people who you featured if they know of other articles that would be a fit gives those people a reason to respond to you and it provides you with a never-ending strategy to consistently have others help drive traffic to your site.

If you can get in the habit of mentioning people or brands in your content and then making them aware that they're mentioned, you'll see your traffic spike and, as a result, your email list grow.

Resources mentioned to help grow an owned audience:

- Drip - https://evergreenprofits.com/drip

- Clickfunnels - https://evergreenprofits.com/clickfunnels

- Designrr - https://evergreenprofits.com/designrr

- LeadPages - https://evergreenprofits.com/leadpages

- Teachable - https://evergreenprofits.com/teachable

- OptinMonster - https://evergreenprofits.com/optinmonster

- Wordpress - https://wordpress.org/

- Ideas For Designrr - https://evergreenprofits.com/designrrhowto

How To Drive Traffic To Your Content – The Experts Weigh In

In addition to the loads of experts that we have interviewed on the podcast, we went around and got leading experts to talk specifically how they drive traffic with content.

For many years, we were a content marketing agency. We learned a ton by experimenting along the way.

Today, we've stopped doing agency work, but content marketing is at the backbone of all of our traffic strategies.

Check out what these experts do to get targeted eyeballs to their content. And you know what targeted eyeballs means… it means your life gets A LOT easier when you start selling them something!

Most people don't quite understand "Content Marketing."

I think most people understand the concept…

They realize that content helps them be seen as an authority and that it might help them with the search engines but they don't quite understand how to really scale their business using content marketing.

The truth is that writing blog content is not an "If you build it, they will come" strategy.

You can't simply put up content and expect a ton of eyeballs to just magically appear on it.

It's important that content gets a bit of a "kickstart." You need some way to drive the initial traffic to it, before it starts getting shared.

That initial boost is one of the biggest keys to content marketing success…

40

It's also the point that most new marketers struggle with.

The truth is that there are a countless amount of ways to drive that initial traffic...

...And to prove my point, we reached out to some of our friends who are genius content marketers and asked them what their best strategy is to drive traffic.

Many of these responses will give you actionable process that you can follow right now to kickstart your traffic.

To start, we asked a handful of friends this question:

"What is your best piece of advice for ensuring that someone gets eyeballs on their content?"

We later revised that question in an attempt to get even more detailed responses (more on that in a moment).

Here's the responses we received:

Lewis Howes

Lewis is the author of the Bestseller, The School of Greatness, and host of the podcast by the same name. His podcast, focused on business and personal development, is one of the most popular podcasts on iTunes.

When we asked him the question he gave this response:

"Create something great that adds value and helps a lot of people... Those people will make sure others see it."

@LewisHowes | LewisHowes.com

Sean Vosler

Sean is a marketing consultant and online educator. He's very active on social media and has some massive engagement on his content. We are constantly impressed by the amount of comments Sean gets on Facebook...

Here's what Sean had to say:

"It needs to change your life before it can change someone else's."

We followed up with Sean to clarify and Sean added this:

"It's not worth eyeballs if it doesn't make an impact."

Sean on Facebook | Increase.Academy

Note from the editor:

Both Lewis and Sean make really good points. Content marketing is not about cranking out a ton of content that doesn't add value to people's lives. It's about creating a resource that's valuable for people and is worth sharing.

Too many people just create junk and wonder why no one's looking at it...

Be valuable or your content will never gain traction.

That being said, we wanted to try to solicit some more "step-by-step" type processes that someone could follow after they've created their immensely valuable content.

We opted to change up the question that we asked slightly in order to gain and share some valuable "tactics" that you can employ after your content is already created to generate that "kickstart."

Here's the new question:

"There's a general notion out there in content marketing that 'if you build it, they will come' and that all you need to do to succeed in content marketing is create great content. However, as we know, we need to give the traffic to that content a little kickstart to really get some traction... What is your go-to strategy to jumpstart the traffic to a piece of your content."

We received some amazing responses from this one so get ready to take some notes because you're about to learn how to drive loads of traffic!

Ben Adkins

Ben is someone that we are constantly impressed by. The amount of courses and content his company puts out is mind-boggling.

His company puts out a ton of online training courses and killer marketing tools. He then uses content marketing to drive traffic to it…

Here is his process:

One of the most effective ways that we've been able to get our content in front of our target audience and turn that content into sales is by leveraging Facebook's Boosted Post Feature on our Pages.

A lot of people have complained about boosted post over the past few years. Most of those people don't understand the pure power behind how Facebook has upgraded this ad option.

You need a page with at least 3000 fans for this to be highly effective. The more you have, the cheaper your ads will be right out of the gate.

So this is what we do with every new piece of content.

1) We setup a post on Facebook with a link to our blog post. That post is typically the link and a one sentence comment on what the article contains. We don't go overboard with text. We just comment on it like a normal personal sharing the article on their own timeline would.

2) We boost the post for 7 days at about $10 per day using the targeting and boost options right on our FB Page.

During that period of time the post will "mature" and start to get cheaper clicks. (your most expensive ad click cost usually come within the first 48 hours so it pays to have less of a daily budget until the ad matures and gets engagement. This will drive your cost down per click.)

3) After 7 days we evaluate the boosted post and see how it did.

If it doesn't get a lot of interaction we just stop spending ad dollars on it.

If it does well, we take the same post and boost it again from the ad editor, but this time we set it at an ongoing rate of $10 per day.

4) After a week of doing that we start to inch of the daily budget slowly. This keeps FB's algorithm in check. When most people try to scale an ad they put too much extra money into the ad at once. This actually throws the ad algorithm off and can result in your click cost going up.

By doing this, we get our content in front of our audience for an extremely cheap price. It typically cost us just a few cents a click in highly competitive markets where people are spending a lot more.

@BenAdkins | FearlessSocial.com

Justin Brooke

Justin Brooke is one of the pioneers in content marketing. He is actually one of the first people that we ever heard the concept of "Content Amplification" from.

His blog posts and content over the years has had a huge impact on the way that we do our own marketing for ourselves and our clients.

Here's what Justin had to say:

"I like to pay for eyeballs to my content. The way I look at it, if you're hoping for traffic to your content then it's likely because you believe it will get people to become a lead or buy something.

Or maybe you write for fun? If that's the case, uhmmm… I got nothing for you.

So if you think your content will turn readers into leads and sales, why not just quickly pay for people to show up? Instead of waiting for the Google gods to bless you or trying to win the "I went viral" lottery, just pay a few bucks and see what happens.

If wehad zero dollars, my next best thing would be to write content that we know a specific group of people would love. For example, find a specific Facebook group. Study what they talk about for a few weeks. Then create a piece of content that they would go nuts over. For example, if it's a FB group about gardening you could write "We Asked 1,000 Gardeners for Their Biggest Secrets And All Of Them Had This One In Common." No gardener in their right mind is going to see that as spam, let alone be able to resist reading.

In summary, write stuff that people can't resist wanting to read. And if you don't know how, then you just haven't done enough market research to know what they find irresistible."

@JustinBrooke | DMBIOnline.com

Navid Moazzez

Navid was actually one of the very first guests on the Multiply Authority podcast. We talked about the concept of "virtual summits," a term and concept that Navid has helped pioneer. He's been featured in places like Forbes, Entrepreneur, The Huffington Post, Business Insider, Yahoo Finance, Ramit Sethi's I Will Teach You To Be Rich, Eofire, So Money, Neil Patel and many more. He has a mission to show you what is REALLY working to build your profitable online business, wherever you're starting. Find out more about his courses, summits, and expertise at http://www.navidmoazzez.com.

Here's what he had to say:

"One of the most powerful books I've ever read was Dale Carnegie's How to Win Friends and Influence People. And one of the best quotes in that book is, "Remember that a person's name is to that person the sweetest and most important sound in any language."

That goes for seeing your name in print or on a computer screen, too! EVERYONE likes to see nice things written about them. So, write great things about great people and let them know about it.

When we write an epic blog post, epic guide, or other piece of content, we include quotes and examples from other influencers. This strategy helps on several fronts:

1. It makes the content better for the reader. More anecdotes and examples means more illustrations of the principle or concept we are trying to convey

2. It lends authority. When you quote influencers, there's an "Oprah" effect that makes you seem more of an expert or authority yourself

3. It makes it more likely influencers will share the content. If someone tagged you on Twitter and said, "Hey, I mentioned you on my blog today! Want the link?" we bet you'd say "Yes." OF COURSE you want to see what someone else said... and you'd probably want to share it, too.

4. It provides value for the influencer. We always include a link back to the influencer's site so they will benefit from the inbound link. Everyone likes inbound links from valuable content, so it's an easy way to provide value for someone we'd like to build a relationship with.

Of course, do this in an authentic and valuable manner — don't just stuff a bunch of names into a post. That just looks stupid.

Make it valuable for the reader AND the influencer, reach out to the influencer via email or social media, and tell them they were included in your post. Ask if they want a link. If it's a well-written, valuable piece of content, they're probably going to share it.

So here's a challenge to you: The next blog post you write, include examples, quotes, or anecdotes from 3 influencers in your niche. If you include us, tag us on social media or send an email, and let us know you took our advice. Who knows? Maybe we'll share your post!" @NavidMoazzez | navidmoazzez.com

Paul Clifford

Paul Clifford is the founder of several content marketing tools, including Kudani and Designrr. Both are tools that we use quite frequently here at Evergreen Profits. (Paul gave us a coupon code for Kudani – If you grab Kudani, use the code "MATT30" for 30% off the package that you choose.)

Paul actually wrote the book, Content Marketing for dummies and practices what he preaches, using proven content marketing strategies to drive traffic to his various software platforms.

Here's Paul's favorite strategy:

"The easiest free way of doing this is by creating a quality curated article from trending and relevant content that solves your audience's problems. Here is an outline of the process; first incorporate influencer curation into your content. By curating a paragraph or some key points from a post written by an influencer in your market, you are achieving 3 things.

One – you're giving your reader great value by selecting and delivering the best solutions for their problems. Two; You are giving a backlink and traffic to the influencer your curated from. Three – Better Google results as your post will rank faster.

Kudani makes the process of finding trending content easier and helps you curate content providing the correct attribution back to the source. The last big benefit is you're creating a longer article of a handful of curated elements which enable you to produce longer and more engaging articles. (Longer post generate more SEO and traffic)

Now comes the interesting part By now you will have curated an article from several influencers and have the opportunity to reach out to them and ask them for a mention or tweet. Most will appreciate you sending them traffic and links and will gladly tweet your post to their audience. If you have 5 influencers mentioned – then you have 5 times more potential for traffic '

(Also check out this in-depth explanation of all of the ways that we use Designrr here: https://evergreenprofits.com/designrrhowto)

@Paul__Clifford | Kudani.com

Nick Loper

Nick Loper probably has a larger mental database of ways to make money than anyone we've ever met… That's because he runs Side Hustle Nation, a site and podcast about the various ways that people make extra income on the side.

His blog and podcast have become huge resources for anyone looking for "side hustle" income streams, mostly due to the content marketing strategies that he employs.

Here's his best tip:

"So it's actually similar to the round-up post strategy employed here, but the most effective posting strategy I've found this year to get a lot of eyeballs is the "Epic List Post." My two most popular posts of the year are "The 134 Best Udemy Courses for Entrepreneurs, Freelancers, and Side Hustlers" and "The Sharing Economy: 200+ Ways to Make Extra Money in Your Spare Time".

These posts probably both took north of 40 hours to research, write, and format, but they're so juicy people can't help but share them. It's not like 5 Things I Learned About Entrepreneurship From My Dentist or The Top 10 Things to do in an Francisco … it's like trying to build something an order of ma gnitude bigger.

Plus, when you hit publish, you automatically have 100 people to message — as I'm sure you'll o with this post — and say "Hey, I featured you in my latest articl ." That's *100x* more people who might like to share your work than or a "regular" post."

@nloper | SideHustleNation.cc n

Tony Teegarden

Tony is the host of the "Turn Your Problems into Profits" podcast. He teaches his clients how to generate high-paying clients from your blog. Not only does Tony use content marketing, he uses it to generate clients that pay him upwards of $6,000 to $10,000 for consulting and coaching.

Here's Tony's advice:

"Wrap Your "Pill" In a Piece of Cheese…

If you try and give a dog a pill that they need, they usually won't take it and spit it out. But if you wrap it in a piece of cheese, they'll scarf it right down.

Far too many people try to serve up content around what they think people need rather than what they actually want.

Everyone wants to get, keep, or get rid of something in their lives.

When your content implies it's something that can help them get something, keep something or et rid of something…they're way more likely to consume it."

@ateegarden | TonyTeegarden om

Stefan James

Stefan James runs Project Life Mastery, a blog and YouTube channel about becoming a better you. He discusses topics like business growth, fitness, personal fulfillment and more. He makes over 7-figures per year throu

gh his Amazon book sales, course sales, affiliate marketing, investments and more... And he lays it all out in his monthly "goal reports".

Over time, Stefan has built a massive platform that has made generating traffic pretty easy for him.

Here's what he had to say:

"My strategy for getting eyeballs to my content is nothing extraordinary. Just simply ensuring that my content is extremely high quality, has a benefit-driven headline that captures attention, is optimized the best it can be for SEO, and then shared to everyone and anyone that can benefit. When you're an influencer and already have a following, it's easy to get eyeballs to it – as I simply just share to my following on Facebook, Twitter, Instagram, Snapchat, e-mail list, etc… and then if the content is really valuable, others will share it for you and the rest will take care of itself."

@StefanJames23 | ProjectLifeMastery.com

Parham Nabatian

Parham is one of the few people who we've seen do extremely well using LinkedIn Pulse as their content marketing platform of choice. Parham focuses on building his personal brand as well as the brand of his agency through carefully crafted and researched content over on LinkedIn.

His branding and web development agency, Infinite Communication, have helped well-known companies become even larger of a presence online through creative branding, web development, and even through content marketing strategy. Parham is a guy to pay attention to in the marketing world. He's a thought leader and branding expert.

Here's his advice:

"When my content does supremely well is when it emotionally connects with people – it not only teaches people something valuable but also makes them feel empowered by reading it. That is why I write the content for my circle, because if my circle connects to it and finds it valuable then I know th y will be the initial wave of people who will share, like or promote the content.

Before I hit publish, I message ny close colleagues to view, like, and share my content right away be ause if the content doesn't stay on people's feed then it won't hav as many eyeballs. Another valuable factor is that I have strong rela onships with a few influencers – so when they share my content th # of views double or triple.

Lastly my secret sauce is using ι personal photo of myself as the header photo – again it's about onnection and it does it much better than a generic stock photo, wh h I think actually turns people off."

Parham on LinkedIn | ThisIsIn nite.com

Tom VanBuren

Tom is the head of content marketing for the brilliant content re-syndication tool, Edgar. Edgar itself is actually an amazing tool to generate traffic to your content. It allows you to load up a library of all of your content and it will continually re-post that content over and over again on social media at set intervals, ensuring that your older content constantly gets new eyeballs.

Here's what Tom from Edgar had to say about getting eyeballs on content:

"Social media promotions are great and all, because you can share something again and again over time to keep a regular trickle of visitors coming in, but when you want a surge of traffic to a new piece of content, it's hard to beat email. Every week, we send out a newsletter promoting our most recent blog posts, and we reliably get a huge traffic bump on the days we send them out! (Plus, all those readers means a big surge of social shares, too.)

This is why building an email list should be one of your top priorities as a content marketer. Whether you're offering a free download, a product trial, access to a webinar, or anything else in exchange for email addresses, every person who joins your list is a person who has demonstrated interest in what you have to say. As you add more of those people to your list over time and regularly send them your new content, you can increasingly drive more traffic, get more social shares, and develop an eager fan base of subscribers who want more of what you have to offer!"

@trvanburen | MeetEdgar.com

Dai Manuel

Dai Manuel is a lifestyle mentor and personal fitness educator. He uses content marketing to attract people to his training and his books. He is a speaker and has been featured all over in the media in the fitness world.

His blog and the content that he puts out is a large driver for the traffic he receives and the success he has had.

Here are Dai's words of wisdom:

"My typical strategy is to connect with like-minded people in my tribe. Over the years I've built some online communities and I continue to nurture those relationships to this day. When I write a new piece of content I share on my typical channels including Twitter, IG, Facebook, Snapchat etc... but I tend to find some of the best shares and traffic is from the communities I've mentioned above."

@DaiManuel |

Pat Flynn

Pat has one of the most popular blogs and podcasts on the topic of internet marketing and growing passive income. Through selling courses, affiliate marketing, podcast sponsorships, and book publishing, Pat has built a 7-figure per year online marketing empire.

All of this success is a direct result of Pat's content marketing efforts on his blog, podcast, and YouTube.

When we interviewed Pat Flynn, we had a little discussion about traffic strategies.

Pat is a big proponent of building relationships and then leveraging those relationships into traffic.

Here's some quotes that were pulled from the interview:

"Getting links from other sites is important. There's a couple of ways to do that. Obviously, just writing great content on your site so that it gets picked up... but also building relationships with other people... Or retweeting other people who look up to you on Twitter and sharing other people's articles on Facebook and connecting with them, sending quick messages and getting on their radar."

Pat also recommends roundup posts…

"Another thing to do to get on people's radar is these roundup posts where you pull a list of maybe 20 of the top most influential people in your niche and have them answer one question. More than likely they're going to share that because they're featured on it."

Finally, Pat also mentioned that just posting all of his content to Twitter has been a really effective traffic source for him.

@PatFlynn | SmartPassiveIncome.com

Jay Baer

Jay is a content marketing thought leader. He's also someone that we've learned a ton from, especially in the area of content repurposing. He did a show called "Jay Today" over on his Convince And Convert blog that he then repurposed in something like 10 different ways to make sure he was getting eyeballs on the content from everywhere. It was amazing and taught us a huge lesson in the power of repurposing your content.

Jay has advised more than 700 brands since getting started in online marketing in 1993. He is also the New York Times best-selling author of five books, the most retweeted person in the world among digital marketers, the second-most influential person in content marketing, and a certified BBQ judge.

Here's his killer tip: "Take your best content ideas and turn them into Slideshare presentations. Slideshare is one of the best opportunities for content exposure, and has the advantage of built-in lead generation tools." @jaybaer | convinceandconvert.com

Joe Pulizzi

Joe is the creator of the Content Marketing Institute, an absolutely brilliant website all about content marketing. He is one of the leading experts and educators in the world on the topic. He's also the author of my personal favorite book on the topic, Content Inc.

Here's Joe's quick piece of advice:

"Yes, spend about 5 times more on promotion than creation (paid and free).

You are correct, if you build it, they won't necessarily come."

@joepulizzi | contentmarketinginstitute.com

Arthur Tubman

Arthur is the founder of D4Y F and Builder, an agency that works with clients to create marketing campaigns which allows them to scale their businesses. In 2009, ne was part of a launch called Free Blog Factory, that was part of a web based reality show featured on front page of Orange County R gister. He worked with celebrity talent like Hulk Hogan and Alf nso Robiero and big companies to create more conversions in the businesses.

Arthur reached out to us becau e he had a really killer traffic strategy that wasn't yet mentioned in th s post and wanted to share it with you... And we are so glad he d d because this is some killer stuff!

Here is what he had to say:

"We build community pages o Facebook (not to be confused with brand pages). Things like a cor munity of people that love talking about their favorite show, or do g breed, or music genre versus a public profile, like Petco or Ta lor Swift. Typically, on average, a Facebook page will have about 10% reach rate per week, and an engagement rate that is too low to count. Most people do not put enough emphasis on interacting with their fans and providing high quality content that the audience loves to consume. Most of our pages average a minimum Reach of 200-300% of the total page likes per week, and an engagement rate of at least 80%."

Here is an image of insights for a page in the entertainment niche with just shy of 325,000 fans that Arthur sent me:

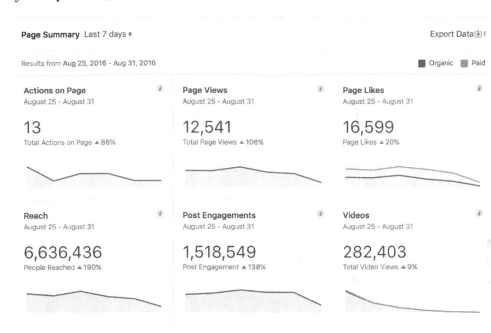

This page has created over 1 million pageviews to our content site just in the last 7 days. And 2 of the top 4 most shared articles ever for the broad keyword on BuzzSumo.

This is the traffic on the site in the last 22 hours. We use a tool called Siphon Cloud, and its pretty epic, because what most people don't know is that a lot of traffic is not only fake and bot traffic, but not tracked by google (private, vpn, trac phones, etc). Many times 2-4 times more traffic then that tracked by google analytics... The beauty of our strategy is that we only have 11% fake traffic, compared to the average of 25-35% because our traffic builds real, and legitimate communities, people want to interact with!

@ArthurTubman | D4YBrandBuilder.com

Matt Wolfe

Matt's favorite strategy to make sure that he get eyeballs on his blog posts is actually multi-part.

First, in every single blog post that he write, he make sure to talk about and link to a few businesses or people. He mentions people that inspired the post or that he pulled excerpts from and then link back to their websites.

He then shoot a message to these people on Twitter and tag them when sharing the post on Facebook. This makes them aware that he is talking about them and, hopefully, encourages them to share the post (people love when others are talking about them).

Next, he create a "boost post" on his Facebook fan page, targeting an interest that he thinks would enjoy the post. Usually his boost post is between $10 and $15 for a 3-day boost. He only blog about once per week, so this process only costs between $40 and $60 per month.

Finally, he mails his list with a link to the post.

Obviously, everyone doesn't have a list yet... Make sure you're always building one and this step will become a bigger and bigger portion of your traffic over time ...

Matt has outlined a step-by-step of my favorite strategy in this content curation post: https://evergreenprofits.com/contentcurationpost

@MattRWolfe | EvergreenProfits.com

Note from the editors:

After rounding up these responses from our friends, we wanted to dive deeper and find some common answers from some other big names in the marketing world.

Here's some other responses that we came up in our research...

Tim Ferriss

Tim doesn't really talk about marketing tactics much. He's much more about deconstructing habits of people. However, back in 2009, he gave a presentation at Wordcamp called "How to build a high-traffic blog without killing yourself." In this video, he divulged some of the tactics that he used to get some initial traffic to his blog.

At about 20 minutes in, Tim talks about SEO.

When he writes his first draft, he ignores SEO completely... He then goes back, uses the Google keyword tool to find popular keywords, and then replaces words throughout his posts with more highly-searched keywords.

Tim also suggests StumbleUpon as a very effective and cheap traffic source to kick off the blog (about 23:50 in). This post is from 2009 and we haven't heard much about StumbleUpon recently... However, that doesn't mean that it's not still an effective strategy. Definitely something to play around with!

Finally, Tim suggests writing about evergreen topics instead of posting items related to current events. Evergreen content will only pick up traction over time while news-based content will fade quickly.

@tferriss | FourHourWorkWee .com

Gary Vaynerchuk

We dug and dug to try to find a concrete traffic strategy from Gary. He's obviously a big fan of social media and putting his face everywhere. In one video that we found (which you can watch here: https://evergreenprofits.com/garyv) he discussed how Facebook was a huge traffic driver for him...

Here's what he had to say:

"Facebook is actually probably one of the biggest drivers of content awareness outside of itself to other destinations in the world right now..."

"I have a pretty big foundation of 150,000 fans on that page, but there's people that I've seen post content that have 800 fans, and enough people shared it and enough people liked it, enough people commented on it and shared it not only within Facebook but outside of it, that it created a fire. Facebook is content awareness infrastructure..."

"I think it's one of the singular best ways, and so I would highly recommend making an investment in Facebook fan pages, recognizing the distribution opportunities that it creates for content you're putting outside of its network."

@garyvee | ask.garyvaynerchuk.com

James Altucher

James is currently one of my favorite authors. His "Choose Yourself" books are phenomenal. He's got a great blog and a couple of awesome podcasts… So he's constantly needing to find ways to drive new traffic to blog posts. Luckily, he's written quite a few times on the topic.

Here's some tips I've picked up from James:

"1. Comment on every blog related to your site. be helpful and don't be annoying.

2. Syndicate your content to the top blogs in your niche.

3. Create a fan page for your niche and share your stuff there.

4. Self-publish a book in your niche.

5. Answer questions on Quora.

6. Link with others in your niche on LinkedIn."

From the blog post: How To G t Traffic To Your Site

In another post, he dug deeper n the topic… The idea is to build a platform of people who pay att ntion to what you do… Then traffic becomes easy.

Here's a quote where he furthe elaborates on syndication:

"Syndicate – write for other bl gs. Write for the Huffington Post, or the top blogs in whatever field ou are interested in. I've syndicated my material on at least 10 othe popular blogs and tried to syndicate on others that said, "no" (famo sly, the Harvard Business School blogs where they passed aroun my material and I saw at the bottom of the email chain, "And yet ar ther".)

Do this consistently for a year. You will get a following. Note it won't be a big enough following to g nerate a good living from ads. But it will give you a launching pad t think about other business ideas. Someone once told me: "all yo need is 1000 true fans to build a business". So you will get you 1000 true fans. And then you can decide what to do with them."

The above quote is from "How Do You Get Traction From Your Blog."

@jaltucher | jamesaltucher.con

Content Marketing Recap

Here's some quick bullets to help distill some of the common responses about driving traffic.

- Focus on creating high quality content first. This is the most important rule. If it's not valuable people won't read it, they won't share it, and it will never pick up traction.

- Share your new piece of content on social media… Twitter, Facebook, and LinkedIn at the very least.

- Don't be afraid to pay to get the initial eyeballs. Facebook boosted posts are a relatively inexpensive but effective method for amplifying your content to get the initial traction.

- Mention others in your posts or curate other's content. You can then tell people they've been mentioned and they are more likely to share.

- Create a community of people that are interested in helping each other out. Tap that network to help share with each new blog post.

- Create the occasional roundup post (like this one), contributors are likely to share the post, creating a highly viral piece of content.

- Make sure you are always focused on building a mailing list so that you can easily bring people back to the site in the future.

- Repurpose the content that you create on other platforms to create new opportunities to be discovered.

Follow those rules along with the more detailed steps from the experts above and you will always be able to kickstart and drive a large spike of initial visitors to your content, leading to new opt-ins and more sales.

Drive Traffic And Grow Your Brand Through Content Curation

Now that we've gone down the vein of content marketing a bit, one of our content "hacks" is content curation. Most people get this all wrong and think that just means you're stealing other people's content. WRONG!

When you do content curation right, you are creating a hell of a win-win-win for everyone. Your reader wins by reading different perspectives about the topic you're writing about. The content creator that you are leveraging is getting exposure in many new ways. And YOU are winning by leveraging other content and adding your own commentary and insights to it. winning!

And another benefit is this is a great way to kick start some free, organic traffic to your site. It gets the ball moving if you have a limited budget. But if you do have some ad budget, then you can really start cranking traffic to these content pieces.

Here's exactly how we curate content effectively. Use this method and you will be a content powerhouse in no time and people will be wondering how you produce so much day in and day out...

We are big proponent of content curation.

It's one of the best ways to get fantastic content on your site, generate a ton of value for people, and give a ton of traffic.

However, so many people do content curation completely wrong.

It's not uncommon to see someone just repost someone else's blog post word-for-word on their blog with a tiny sentence stating "Originally posted on some other blog."

What follows is a strategy that utilizes other people's content to create additional value for your readers, benefits the original content creator, and encourages other people to share your content.

Following this process will also build your list so you can create your own traffic "at will" in the future.

This is a process that we often create and systematize for our clients.

Step 1: Curate great content on your blog

In this step, we're going to think of a topic that's going to interest our group. For a "content marketing" blog, I might pick a topic like "10 ways to generate content without actually creating it yourself".

A great place to get some ideas for blog content is BuzzSumo… Simply type in your main keyword and see what's getting shared the most.

Here's a list of ideas from typing in "Content Generation":

Now it's time to start curating.

Find somewhere in the range o 7 to 10 different blogs that discuss this topic.

I did a quick search on Google or "Content Marketing Blogs" and this blog post was one of the fi st...

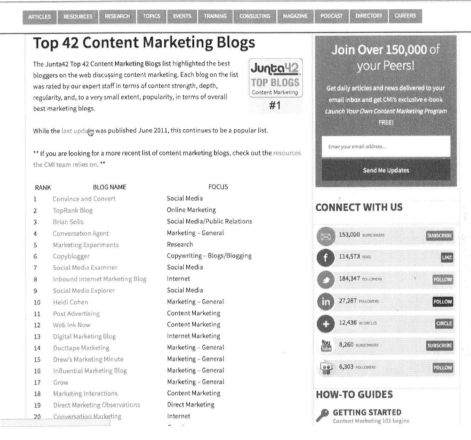

(From Content Marketing Institute)

We are pretty sure we can find some pretty killer blog posts to curate from some of those resources…

Now, find a blog post from each of those sites that best responds to the topic that you choose above.

Here is an article Convince and Convert (Rank #1 on the list above) that we might include:

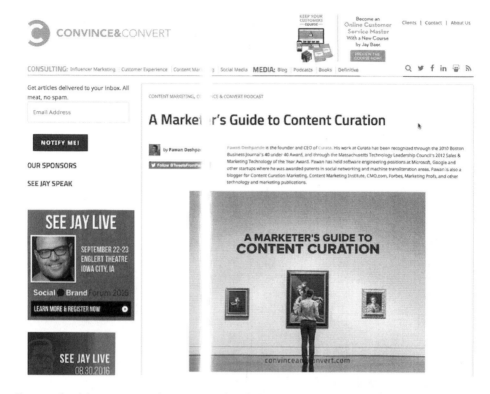

Create the blog post and quote ...ach of the blog posts that you just found. A little bit of commenta...y to each post about why it fits in this blog post.

If we were to curate a post like...he one above, it would probably look something like this:

"Content Curation" is one of th... quickest and easiest ways to get high-value content on your site... without actually writing most of the content yourself. Pawan Deshp...nde put together a phenomenal guide on how marketers can do conte...t curation correctly. Read the article here.

We'd probably go slightly mor... in-depth with my description... But that gives you a good idea.

Repeat that 6 to 9 more times f...r each of your resources...

Make sure that you link out to each of these blog posts and give attribution to the original writer.

As a quick note, we use a tool called Kudani to help streamline the process of finding content to curate, posting the content, and properly attributing the content. It's a killer tool and, if you grab it, use the coupon code "MATT30" to get 30% off. This isn't a pitch for Kudani… we just wanted to be transparent that we do leverage that tool to help us find what to post. More about that tool here: https://evergreenprofits.com/curation

Step 2: Spread the word

Now it's time to hit Twitter, Facebook, and LinkedIn… we like to hit all three because different people seem to hang out on different platforms, and we want to make sure that the people we mention in the post are aware of the post.

When we share the post on Facebook and LinkedIn, we'll tag every person that was mentioned in the blog post.

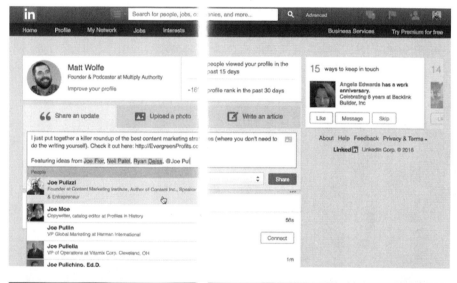

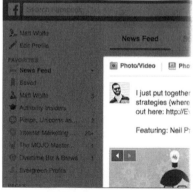
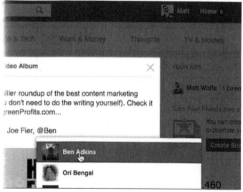

When we share the post on Twitter, we will create a new tweet for every single person mentioned in the post, letting them know that they've been featured.

Finally, if there are contact forms on the blogs that you mentioned, shoot the original author a quick email with a link to your post. Let them know that you featured them in a "best of" type post.

Ideally, at least half of the people that you mentioned will turn around and do a quick tweet or share of the post. People love it when others talk about their work and like to share the fact that others are talking about it…

Here's a post of mine that Sujan Patel of ContentMarketer.io shared of mine… He has over 30k followers and gave my site a nice little spike in Twitter traffic.

Sujan Patel @sujanpatel · 17 ct 2015
How To Build An Authority B g From Scratch multiplyauthority.com/how-to-
build-a... via **@MattRWolfe**

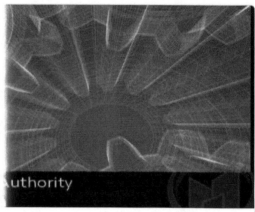

How To Build An Authori   Blog From Scratch - Multiply Authority
A step-by-step explanatio of how this website will become an Authority
Blog within the next few m nths.
multiplyauthority.com

 ♺ 8   ♥ 9   • • •

Step 3: Build a retargeting audience.

Now it's time to make sure that we turn this newfound traffic into people that return to the site over and over again.

Start by ensuring that you're building a retargeting audience in both Facebook and Google Adwords.

Both Facebook and Google will provide you with a little snippet of code that you can paste into the code of your blog, allowing you to use your previous visitors as targets for advertising.

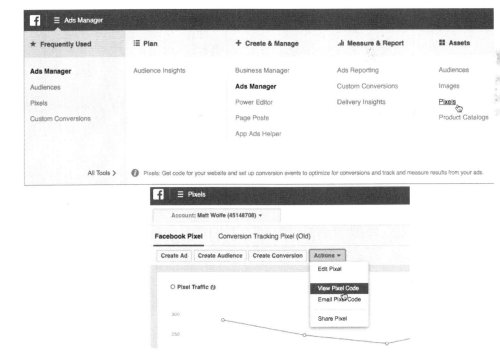

Now, whenever you create a new blog post, link to it from your Facebook fan page and simply "Boost" the post.

Evergreen Profits
Published by Matt Wolfe [?] · ıgust 8 at 5:54pm · 🌐

One of the best things that you ca n do to grow your business is to put out high-quality and informative cont t that builds you and your business as the true expert...

The problem is that most people cus on putting content on their own sites... It's a much better use of ti e and content to leverage existing large brands and their site / platform...

We put together this simple little uide to help you get published on some of the biggest sites in the world!

How To Get Featured O The World's Biggest Websites

The Huffington Post. Business Insid Mashable. Inc.com. When it comes to big name resources, spanning a variety tegories, these publications are the cream of the crop. As a writer, company ow er, or rketing professional, you know one...

EVERGREENPROFITS.COM

Boost Post

👍 Like   💬 Comment   ➤ hare   ▾

🔘 Alan Beilstein and Chris Martinez

Write a comment...   📷   ☺

Press Enter to post.

When you boost the post, you can choose specific targets… Make sure you're targeting the people that have previously been to your website.

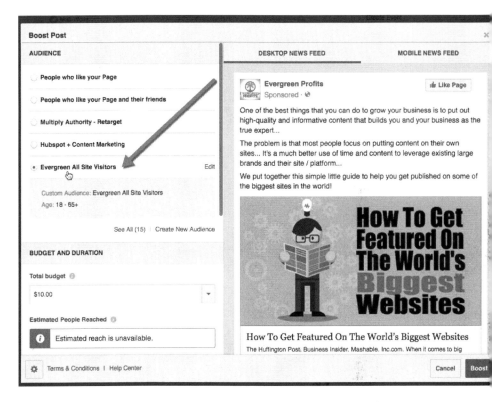

This gives people the impression that you put out a ton of content and spend a ton of money on advertising. It's amazing for building your brand and driving repeat traffic back to the blog.

Step 4: Collect emails from your blog.

Install Thrive Leads... That's the tool that we love and use on this blog as well as on MultiplyAuthority.com.

My personal favorite uses are the slide-in tool and the exit-intent lightbox.

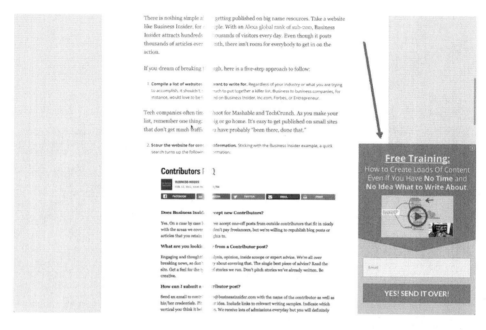

The slide-in opt-in form slides in from the bottom right of the screen once someone scrolls at least 1% into the content. This is really effective and not overly-intrusive.

The exit-intent lightbox is the popup that appears when someone moves their cursor away from the browser like they are about to leave the site. These work to grab visitors right before they are about to leave.

Make sure you have something valuable to give away for free, in exchange for the email.

Step 5: Contact your new audience.

It's time to bring your newly created audiences back to the site.

Each time you put a new blog post live, mail your list about the new post and then create a Facebook "Boosted Post" that targets past visitors.

We will also often boost the post again to a "cold" audience…

We will find an interest target on Facebook that we think will enjoy the post and target them with our ads. This brings some new people to the site that could potentially opt-in as well as new people that will get added to your retargeting list.

Step 6: Repeat…

You can use the process over and over again, targeting new blogs and resources with each new post.

Try to use new blogs each time. Other bloggers will, most likely, share your post the first time you do this but, if you do it too often, they'll probably become immune to this technique and stop sharing. So find some fresh blogs each time.

Fairly *unestablished blogs* work fantastic for this because they tend to be the MOST flattered when someone else is talking about them. Always try to include one or two blogs that are somewhat "undiscovered" and watch those people become your biggest evangelists!

You can also create "roundup" posts where you send the same question to 50 different people and ask for an answer… Create a post that rounds up all the responses and links back to their website… These get a TON of shares but are a little more time-consuming to build. You will see a post just like this on Evergreen Profits next week. It will make an excellent case study.

Hire someone to write original content once you've got an audience built up. This will further establish credibility, build trust, and help with SEO.

Final Thoughts & What's Next

That's it! That's the entire process that we run through when trying to help our client's blogs get some initial traction.

The hardest part about getting a blog going is that initial traffic to the site. Creating posts like the ones described here for the first couple of weeks will give your blog a kickstart and get a lot of people talking about it right out of the gate.

Let's Go Deeper

We hope you enjoyed this deep dive into how we run traffic for our business. The key here is to take at least ONE of the strategies and put it into use. Start planning **right now**.

And remember, these traffic strategies work for not only your own offers, but for affiliate offers, too. It doesn't matter your niche or if you are an online business or brick and mortar, you can make this work.

If you want to really dive in deeper and scale things with a step-by-step plan, you should watch this video and read this quick page. Just go here: **https://evergreenprofits.com/trafficvideo**

Thank you VERY much for reaching this far. We appreciate you and would love to hear what you think.

Just send us a message here and let us know! Go here and you'll start a chat with us: **https://evergreenprofits.com/trafficquestions**

We appreciate you and are looking forward to growing your traffic together!

Matt Wolfe and Joe Fier
Founders of Evergreen Profits
Hosts of the Hustle & Flowchart Podcast